Ten Poems about Trains

RETURN

ex libris

Candlestick Press

Published by:
Candlestick Press,
Diversity House, 72 Nottingham Road, Arnold, Nottingham NG5 6LF
www.candlestickpress.co.uk

Design and typesetting by Craig Twigg

Printed by Bayliss Printing Company Ltd of Worksop, UK

Selection and Introduction © Jonathan Davidson, 2023

Cover illustration © Gail Brodholt
https://gailbrodholt.com/

Candlestick Press monogram © Barbara Shaw, 2008

© Candlestick Press, 2023

ISBN 978 1 913627 26 3

Acknowledgements

The poems in this pamphlet are reprinted from the following books, all by permission of the publishers listed unless stated otherwise. Every effort has been made to trace the copyright holders of the poems published in this book. The editor and publisher apologise if any material has been included without permission, or without the appropriate acknowledgement, and would be glad to be told of anyone who has not been consulted.

Thanks are due to all the copyright holders cited below for their kind permission.

Jonathan Davidson, poem first appeared in this pamphlet. Maura Dooley, *Explaining Magnetism* (Bloodaxe Books, 1991) www.bloodaxebooks.com. Helen Dunmore, *Counting Backwards: Poems 1975-2017* (Bloodaxe Books, 2019) www.bloodaxebooks.com. David Hart, *Running Out* (Five Seasons Press, 2006) by kind permission of Five Seasons Press. Deepankar Khiwani, *The Bloodaxe Book of Contemporary Indian Poets*, ed. Jeet Thayil (Bloodaxe Books, 2008) by kind permissions of the Estate of Deepankar Khiwani. Cynthia Kitchen, *Marigolds Grow Wild on Platforms: An Anthology of Railway Poetry*, ed. Peggy Poole (Cassell Illustrated, 1996) by kind permission of the author. Ian McMillan, *To Fold the Evening Star: New & Selected Poems* (Carcanet Press, 2016). Graham Mort, *Visibility: New and Selected Poems* (Seren, 2007) by kind permission of the author.

All permissions cleared courtesy of Dr Suzanne Fairless-Aitken
c/o Swift Permissions swiftpermissions@gmail.com

Where poets are no longer living, their dates are given.

Contents   **Page**

Introduction   *Jonathan Davidson*   5

Happiness on the First Train   *Ian McMillan*   7
from Barnsley to Huddersfield

To Lethe on the 8.10   *Graham Mort*   8

Night Train to Haridwar   *Deepankar Khiwani*   9

'I like to see it lap the Miles'   *Emily Dickinson*   10

Timetable   *David Hart*   11

Then I think how the train   *Helen Dunmore*   12

Steam Engine, at Arley   *Jonathan Davidson*   13

Strangers on a Train   *Cynthia Kitchen*   14

Backwards into   *Maura Dooley*   15
Wakefield Westgate

From a Railway Carriage   *Robert Louis Stevenson*   16

Introduction

Many people have spent a good deal of time over the last two hundred years travelling on trains. From the comforting warmth of a railway carriage, imaginations have spooled out as travellers have enjoyed a front-row seat in the 'cinema of life'. Robert Louis Stevenson set the tone with his poem, 'From a Railway Carriage', and poems by Ian McMillan, Graham Mort and Maura Dooley continue the tradition. They are carried through a world of fields, houses and factories, always observing and recording. How powerfully do trains connect us to our own histories, tracks coming together or branching off.

Studying our fellow travellers also whiles away the hours. What love, what hope, what happiness those others secretly carry as they are rocked in the cradle of the first train of the day. What regrets come with the unscheduled halt or delayed departure, as Deepankar Khiwani notes. And how easy to fall in love with a stranger, as Cynthia Kitchen possibly suggests in her poem. And then of course there's the machinery of movement. Emily Dickinson was surely an early enthusiast for high-functioning transportation engineering. My goodness, did she admire a steam locomotive! And as a man brought up in Didcot, industrial south Oxfordshire's premier railway town, I am something of a 'steam-hound' myself, my nose twitching at the scent of hot oil and burning anthracite.

Finally, we mustn't forget the potential for train travel to take us back in time, returning us to our first journeys. As poems by David Hart and Helen Dunmore remind us, trains are part of our 'collective imagination', and they make poetry happen. And while not all railways remain, and not every return ticket gets used, still the flicker of memory is constantly refreshing. Always the same journey, but never the same train…

Jonathan Davidson

Happiness on the First Train from Barnsley to Huddersfield

The happiness creeps up on you,
in the dark train as we stop at Dodworth,

then Silkstone Common, then Penistone,
and some people are sleeping and sleeping

is a sort of happiness, and those three men
who are always on this train are talking

and talking is a form of happiness, and I
am looking, and looking is a kind of

happiness. Then the train pulls out
of Penistone Station, across that impossibly

beautiful viaduct that I can never
remember the name of, and the light

is arriving in the sky as if by slow train,
and now I can remember the name

of the viaduct and the name
of the viaduct is Happiness,

Happiness high across the slowly
lightening fields.

Ian McMillan

To Lethe on the 8.10

A weak dawn drowns all England under mist;
this train rocks us in its glass cradle
against the track where steel wheels hiss,
a slick of water glimmers on the pylons' cable.

Trees stand out as skeins of blackened wire,
the windows show us staring at our faces;
mist spreads, choking out the sun's ash-fire,
the stations' names christen nameless places.

That young couple are joined hand in hand,
he sleeps against her and she strokes his head;
he wakes to see pale fogs inhale the land,
white grasses that the winter leaves for dead.

The girder bridge flits by like a lantern show,
the river drinks our lights in darkness far below.

Graham Mort

Night Train to Haridwar

Now past midnight the train stops with a jolt.
Twelve twenty-two. My friend sleeps, unaware
of both this journey and this sudden halt
and gently smiles, as if he could not care;
as if he knew no halt to smile about,
nor ever had a journey he could doubt.

I smile at myself: journey, halts indeed!
I should have been a poet, adrift at sea,
asking the questions that could nowhere lead
except to more uncertain ways to be.
All it could be is engine trouble that
detains us, or some station we stop at.

We should reach there tomorrow by, say, eight.
The first time there, for both me and my friend.
Perhaps an unconscious unacknowledged wait
now hopes its sleepless questioning will end...
I close my eyes, as if to lose my will,
then realise the train is standing still.

In this air-conditioned still compartment, lit
by dim white light, I stretch, then try to see
what is outside the window, but find it
impossible to look outside of me:
there in two panes reflected, clearly seen,
two panes of glass, with a vacuum in between.

Deepankar Khiwani (1971 – 2020)

'I like to see it lap the Miles'

I like to see it lap the Miles —
And lick the Valleys up —
And stop to feed itself at Tanks —
And then — prodigious step

Around a Pile of Mountains —
And supercilious peer
In Shanties — by the sides of Roads —
And then a Quarry pare

To fit its sides
And crawl between
Complaining all the while
In horrid — hooting stanza —
Then chase itself down Hill —

And neigh like Boanerges —
Then — prompter than a Star
Stop — docile and omnipotent
At its own stable door —

Emily Dickinson (1830 – 1886)

Timetable

From Euston's Doric
to Birmingham's Ionic Curzon Street
1838
in five hours
the new religion of railways
was something to take tea by
along the route,
grit in your eye
as *Hercules* goes by
at, believe it or not, 20 mph:
'I saw it!'

Then it was two-and-a-half hours 1854
Euston to Birmingham New Street's
broadest span roof in the world, glass.

Now the new Virgins through New Street
have replaced the old Virgins and

at Moor Street
 the train now standing at platform 2
is running sixty-four years late.
This is due to an Einsteinian blip
between Aberystwyth and Shrewsbury.
We apologise for the late running of this train,
we hope that the coffins, wheelchairs, walking sticks
and flasks of Bovril
have been helpful, we would like to
apologise for the inconvenience caused,
and to welcome you to the 21st century.

David Hart (1940 – 2022)

Then I think how the train

Then I think how the train
from being a far blue point
troubling the slick of track
like thought in the dead of night
with a rack of stations between
the pulse of it and me

suddenly breathes at my back.
The platform stammers
and I see my poems
and see my youth in my poems
look up and back – then I think how the train

argues with a cloud of flowers
and always wins
cutting away with its cargo
leaving me in the carpark.

I tack the tarmac with footmarks
but now the train
switches its tail
shaking the rails,

then I think how the train
was waiting for me, a mushroom
put there for my hand
in the cow-coloured dawn.

That far blue point
how fast it's grown
having visited each one of the rack of stations
and found no one home.

How quick you are, I think to the train,
how near you've come.

Helen Dunmore (1952 – 2017)

Steam Engine, at Arley

Assemblage of steel, deep black paint,
polished but smeary with faint prints
of loving hands, and the lettering drop-
shadowed in yellow and green. All
are amazed. All are delighted, all
stand almost in awe. Steam is sent
heavenward, then stops. The low
whistle amuses those of young
mind, the rest are made quietly
happy by piston and cylinder, by
the low roar of the firebox, the high
hiss of more steam, loving that it
will not be still, cannot be still,
but must still go forward, slowly,
pushing its big weight on fine rails,
stamping its sweet feet to its own tune.

Jonathan Davidson

Strangers on a Train

We are customers on each side
of an Intercity table
you in your corner, I in mine.
We don't talk nor do you
catch my eye as we, delayed
in Birmingham and Crewe, sigh
and turn to newspapers and books
the hidden word; and when you leave
at Wigan without a backward look
taking your rucksack and yawns
I wonder who you were and if
you noticed who I seemed to be.

Cynthia Kitchen

Backwards into Wakefield Westgate

There is a train to anywhere
and you might one day catch it.
At Mirfield, Elsenham, Bridgend or Yatton
I know you by the set of your head,
your determined walk away from me.

Why are you never on my train
which at Bradford and Wakefield
mocks the decision to face forward,
turns me round again, so I can't tell
back from front or past from future?

You look in from the other side
of carriage windows. You disappear in
the crowd at ticket barriers. I see
your cycle leaning in the guard's van.
I need you in the empty seat beside me.

Maura Dooley

From a Railway Carriage

Faster than fairies, faster than witches,
Bridges and houses, hedges and ditches;
And charging along like troops in a battle,
All through the meadows the horses and cattle:
All of the sights of the hill and the plain
Fly as thick as driving rain;
And ever again, in the wink of an eye,
Painted stations whistle by.

Here is a child who clambers and scrambles,
All by himself and gathering brambles;
Here is a tramp who stands and gazes;
And there is the green for stringing the daisies!
Here is a cart run away in the road
Lumping along with man and load;
And here is a mill and there is a river:
Each a glimpse and gone forever!

Robert Louis Stevenson (1850 – 1894)